Shield Your Privacy:
15 Ways To Protect Your
Personal Information

Heather Nickerson

CaryPress International Books

Book design by Tanisa Sharif
Editing by BRG Communications, LLC

CONTENTS

PREFACE

When was the last time you shared information about yourself or a loved one online? That cute photo of you and your family on vacation? Share. The photo of your dog chasing its tail in front of your house? Share. That photo of your new car (and your license plate)? Share.

We share all the time. And we don't give it a second thought. It's commonplace to share personal information online, which then becomes available to complete strangers.

Would you voluntarily want the person in front of you at the coffee shop to see a photo of your child's report card? Probably not. But they just did. Because we share everything.

The truth is, once our information is online, it is very hard to control who has access to it, and it is near to impossible to remove.

Who is controlling our information?
Data aggregators, data archiving sites and online search engines have made it big business to actively store and archive personal information. Some companies even profit from reselling our information.

And we haven't even started to talk about the information you have unknowingly shared. Despite an estimated $114 billion corporate investment worldwide in data security, consumer data breaches happen all the time. Personal Identifying Information (PII) remains the holy grail for cybercriminals given that corporations across a wide range of industries —

including health care, government, and financial services —
store and manage billions of consumer data records.

 In 2018, 2.8 billion consumer data records were exposed at an estimated cost of $654 billion with PII compromised 97% of the time.

- Real names were exposed 91% of the time
- Social Security Numbers and dates of birth were exposed 54% of the time
- Medical records were exposed 46% of the time
- Payment/banking information was exposed 12.2% of the time
- Name and email addresses were exposed 7.8% of the time
- Usernames and passwords were exposed 3.8% of the time

Why is this happening?
The United States lacks a federal law that regulates the collection and use of personal information. The government has approached privacy and security by regulating only certain sectors and types of sensitive information, such as health care and financial.

State laws add to this patchwork, particularly with respect to data breaches. California enacted the first data breach notification law in 2003; 48 other states have since followed and have passed laws that require individuals to be notified if their information is compromised.

The point is, your information is out there. And it is often for sale or used to help others profit. It's up to you to take steps to control and protect it.

INTRODUCTION

My privacy journey started with the birth of my daughter. I've always had a healthy skepticism of social media and its unintended consequences. To this day, I only have a very neglected Facebook profile that I reluctantly signed up for in 2009, and a LinkedIn account I use professionally.

When my daughter was born, I became even more fanatic about protecting our family's privacy. I wanted her to be able to tell her story, in her own words, when she was ready. Lofty goals, I know.

One challenge I encountered was explaining the importance of protecting her and our privacy to family members, who didn't see anything wrong with sharing a few innocent family photos. I put my foot down. You can almost hear the eyerolls. I didn't want to lose control over where her information went once released on Aunt Sally's newsfeed.

But I didn't stop there. I had the same rules for birthday greetings and any other digital messages that could include personal identifying information, such as date of birth, place of birth, full legal name, etc. It is her story, not mine, to tell.

Fast forward five years, and I was suddenly confronted with my mother's untimely and unexpected death. I soon discovered that end-of-life comes with a whole other set of privacy challenges — and I felt just as strongly that the story my mother had lived was hers, and hers alone. I didn't want anyone to co-opt her legacy. (Or worse, her identity.)

Fact: Social Security numbers for those under age 18 and those recently deceased are frequently for sale on the dark web. Why? Because they are easy targets. Parents don't routinely check the credit reports of their children, neither do relatives of the deceased.

It is amazing the information you can lift from an obituary — date and place of birth, college, professional history, next of kin, mother's maiden name, etc. All the information you would need to impersonate the deceased, if you were so inclined.

You can probably guess my stance on my mother's obituary. Queue the eyerolls. I was able to persuade my family to publish a limited version that included non-identifying details about her life. We did not include her full legal name, date of birth or her next of kin.

This was not an easy conversation, nor was it well received. My family thought I was nuts at first. But we all agreed the real threat of identity theft and data privacy meant taking serious precautions.

It's taken me a career in intelligence, the gift of my daughter, the loss of my mother, and countless conversations with friends and colleagues to realize that you need to talk honestly about privacy. No jargon, no acronyms. Just straight forward advice that you can apply to your own life and be in control of your information.

NO SUCH THING AS A FREE APP

Say it with me, "nothing in life is free." This is especially true when it comes to online Applications. Developers design Apps to make money.

How do they make money? By selling your data to marketers, data aggregators, data analytic firms and others who make it their business to piece together enough personal data to be monetized.

A good example of this is the increasingly popular Ovia fertility and ovulation tracker App. Ovia claims to be the most accurate ovulation calculator and fertility tracker on the market, and was rated the number one health App for women and families. Sounds amazing! Wrong. *The Washington Post* revealed how the App makes a profit through advertising and selling user health data, often without their knowledge.

Ovia is not alone. There are hundreds of other "free" Apps that make money off of the sale of user data. For instance, the Realtor.com mobile App tracks your online behavior and shares information about the real estate listings you've viewed.

The Instant Heart Rate: HR Monitor App sends user health data to Facebook. The Weather Live App sends location data and geo-tagged arrival/departure times to various third parties.

And finally, an example that was making headlines — the FaceApp that shows users how they might look when they're older. FaceApp's terms of service give the App makers permission to upload your photo and store it on their server in Russia and grants nearly limitless power to use your photo however they want. No permission needed. You gave them your consent when you downloaded and ran the App.

What can you do?
Always read the fine print before you download and run any App. Understand what data the App will collect from you, how and where the App will store the data it has collected, and how the App and App makers will share the data, if at all.

You have two options if you decide you want to proceed with the App download and install. You could create an account with generic information and use that account solely for online signups and Apps. This account is called a dummy account, and would not be used for any of your day to day correspondence. Or, you could simply use a false name, date of birth, email address and phone number. Do not give away your full legal name, date of birth, email address and phone number. Most Apps do not validate the information they request from you, so you can always use John Doe, at john.doe@gmail.com. There is no reason to give away your valuable data to access a so-called "free" App.

DATA AGGREGATORS ARE TRACKING YOUR EVERY MOVE

Data aggregators — such as WhitePages and Spokeo — are constantly picking up pieces of your personal identity for future use. In technical terms, they gather open source information to build public profiles of individuals that list their contact and demographic information. These sites commonly list people's full legal name, date of birth, address history, phone number, email address and salary information — making it available to the public.

Companies and individuals routinely use information available through data aggregators for legitimate marketing and personal purposes. However, that same information, if used by malicious actors intent on doing you harm, can put your personal safety and information security at risk. It's never been easier to commit criminal activity, such as financial fraud, identity theft or stalking.

In 2017, more than 16.7 million individuals were victims of identity fraud in the U.S. according to a report by Javelin Strategy & Research. Even more disturbing is that stalkers or other criminals with malintent can use data aggregators to learn how to contact you by phone, email or in person at your residence.

What can you do?
You have the ability to request the removal of your information stored on data aggregation websites — also referred to as "opting out" — through written communication and the use of opt-out websites.

Requests are only applicable to the information already stored, and does not prohibit them from collecting the same information in the future. It's on you to make these requests on a regular basis to ensure your information does not reappear on the sites. Remember, if at first you aren't removed, opt-out and opt-out again.

Encourage family members, business partners and roommates to remove their records from data aggregators as well, since their public profiles may inadvertently reveal information about you.

Opt-out checklist:
- Have your personal information prepared before contacting the sites, including full name, aliases, date of birth, phone numbers and address history.
- Some sites may require you to provide a copy of one of your forms of legal identification, such as your driver's license, to verify your identity before complying with your request.

- Some sites may require you to provide a cell phone number or email address to confirm your removal request. You can use your personal email address or create a new email address specifically for this purpose to avoid sharing your contact information.
- Many sites will require you to complete a CAPTCHA when you submit an opt-out request. A CAPTCHA is a tool that websites use to confirm you are not a machine attempting to access information for spam purposes. The CAPTCHA will prompt you to enter text that matches what is displayed in a given image or to select photos from the given options that depict a specific item.

LOOSE DATA IS HARD TO CONTROL

I often hear friends say, "Oh, my information is safe, I only share with friends and family," or, "It doesn't matter, all of my posts auto-delete after 24 hours." I wish it was that simple and I could tell you that auto-deletion prevents your data from being posted online without your knowledge. But it's more complicated.

Let's take the case of Jan and Stan texting each other on a secure messaging App, such as WICKR. (I applaud friends for using WICKR in the first place. More on that in a bit.) Jan texts Stan a photo from a party the other night. Jan has her auto-delete settings set to six hours on WICKR, so as far as she's concerned, in six hours that photo will be history.

Stan really likes the photo and decides to save and share the photo with his friends. Jan has no idea Stan has saved the photo and plans to share it. Jan still believes the photo is set to delete in T-5 hours, but the truth is the photo is now out of her control and could be shared far beyond what she intended.

Sound familiar?

This is a rather benign case, but it helps to explain how photos, texts and other media files can be shared without the original participant's knowledge. It is alarming when you think about the ramifications this has, especially for our children.

For example, Harvard has repeatedly rescinded offers to accepted students based on inappropriate private social media posts that were brought to the attention of the admissions staff. In 2017, ten accepted offers were rescinded when staff was made aware of a private Facebook group in which the students had sent each other memes and messages that were deemed by the Harvard staff to be sexually explicit, anti-Semitic and racially charged.

Almost anything that is digitally sent to another person can be captured and shared by that person. That information can travel the world in a matter of minutes. The hard truth is there's no expectation of privacy if you voluntarily share information about yourself with another person.

What can you do?
The key takeaway here is to think before you share. Do not share anything that you would not want the world to see.

PRACTICE GOOD CYBER HYGIENE

When it comes to establishing privacy for you and your family, stay proactive, and set boundaries and online sharing guidelines with those closest to you.

Open an honest dialogue with your family, friends and colleagues to make sure they understand why practicing good cyber hygiene is important to you. Be specific about what type of information they should and should not share about you and your children.

You might be surprised by the reaction. What may seem like common sense to you might be entirely new to your friend. And it might alert them to their bad cyber habits and help put them on the path to better data security.

What can you do?
Start by asking family and friends to have a conversation

about personal privacy. Here's a list of considerations to help create parameters so everyone feels comfortable and secure.

- Refrain from sharing personal details about you and your children, such as birthdays, nicknames and locations of their activities.
- Do not publicly post photos of your children's faces to prevent members of the general public from identifying them.
- Do not post photos of your children when they are not fully clothed.
- Do not tag extended family members in public posts to prevent the public from identifying the personal accounts of your relatives.
- Disable features that allow members of the public to post on your profile without your approval (if applicable).

With the glaring pressure of the media to contend with, high-profile individuals, such George Clooney, have successfully maintained public social media accounts while preserving their children's anonymity by posting photos that only show the backs of their heads or side profiles.

OVERSHARING IS NOT CARING

I get it. You just summited Mount Kilimanjaro, or you spotted Oprah at dinner, or he (or she) finally popped the question. It's not easy to resist sharing all these "likeable" moments in real-time.

But when you share personal updates and photos on social media, sometimes you are unwittingly sharing information that could be used to cause you harm. For example, a malicious actor might see your vacation photos and know right away that your home is open for "business."

What can you do?
As long as you have a plan and are thoughtful in your approach to sharing personal updates and photos, there are ways to remain secure.

- Post vacation or travel photos only after you have

returned from a trip; this prevents the public from knowing when your residence will be unoccupied while you are away.

- Do not post the names or locations of specific restaurants, cafes, gyms or other venues that you regularly visit. This reveals information about your personal routines that can be used to predict your movements. Request that these businesses refrain from posting photos or tagging you on their public profiles.
- Do not post photos that show unique features of your home or property; these can be used to identify your home address.
- Don't post anything that shows you breaking the rules or the law.

6

PRIVACY SETTINGS EXIST FOR A REASON

A vast amount of information about each of us exists online and much of that information often comes directly from content we share on social media. The good news is if you choose to share, you can optimize the available security settings on these channels to help maintain your privacy and security.

These settings allow you to share content with trusted networks, while protecting personal information from malicious actors who could use the information to harm you — physically, financially or reputationally.

Social media networks and mobile devices are largely configured to automatically make your information public when you sign up for an account. Be aware that making your account private does not delete any content you've already posted, it only limits the visibility of that content.

Similarly, strong privacy settings do not prohibit your trusted network from capturing photos and sharing them on their own accounts. Therefore, never post any content that would be potentially compromising or embarrassing. Think before you post.

What can you do?
Individuals with malicious intent could use your personal information to target you and your family for extortion, identity theft, burglary or other criminal acts.

- Strengthen the privacy and security settings on all your social media accounts to limit the visibility of your personal content.
- Thoroughly review and adjust the privacy and security settings on an ongoing basis, as these settings are updated all the time.
- Use two-factor authentication to sign-in securely and prevent unauthorized access to your accounts.
- Disable the location-sharing information, as adversaries could use your location information to track you.
- Routinely check which electronic devices have been used to access your social media accounts. If there are devices you do not recognize, immediately change the password for that account and report the suspicious login to the particular social media service.
- Use antivirus software to regularly scan your devices for any suspicious programs that could be collecting your information.
- Scrub your contact/friend list at least once a year.
- Connect only with trusted family and friends.

DIFFERENT ACCOUNTS
FOR DIFFERENT REASONS

Maybe you have a lifestyle brand or have made a living out of being a popular influencer. It's okay if you don't want to give that up. You don't have to, but you can take steps to make your information more secure and better protect your privacy.

One easy step is to establish public and private accounts. Think of the public account as the profile that represents your professional persona. The private account is for sharing personal content with your trusted inner circle.

What can you do?
The below guidelines and tips are applicable for setting up a public account, including Instagram, Twitter, Facebook, Flickr and Pinterest.

- Register the account with a unique email address created

solely for this purpose. This email address should be separate from ones used to register your private accounts and should not be used for personal activities.

- Do not allow social media platforms to access the contact list affiliated with your email account.
- Use a unique username that is different from the usernames you use on private accounts, to prevent others from easily identifying your private accounts.
- Do not list your phone number, date of birth, contact information or links to your other social media accounts.
- Turn off geo-tagging features.
- Disable direct messages on your accounts; this will prevent outsiders from sending you unsolicited messages.
- Turn on the two-factor authentication login feature of your accounts to help protect from unauthorized access. (More on that in a bit.)

ALL PASSWORDS ARE NOT CREATED EQUAL

For starters, "password" is not a good password. The same goes for "123456" and "qwerty," all of which were in the top three most hacked passwords of 2019, according to CNN. Other top contenders and equally ill-suited passwords include "111111," "abc123" and "password1."

So, if those are bad passwords, what makes a good password? Ask any cyber security expert and they will recommend you create a password that is between 18 and 26 characters in length, contains at least one upper case letter, one lower case letter, one number and one special character.

That may sound overwhelming. But it's much easier than it sounds.

What can you do?

Think of a short sentence or a familiar phrase, such as "my dog likes to dig dirt." Following the above advice, that simple phrase can easily be turned into a strong password — "MyD0gL1kesToD!gD1rt." Easy to remember, and much harder for a hacker to compromise.

 It takes a supercomputer or botnet a mere .009 seconds to break a simple pin code password like "123456789"

It would take a hacker 4.4 billion years to compromise "MyD0gL1kesToD!gD1rt"

And here's a hot tip. Password managers can help you remember if it's a "!" or a "1." What is a password manager you might ask? Think of it as a digital safe for all your passwords. A password manager will generate, retrieve and keep track of super-long, crazy-random passwords across countless accounts for you, while protecting your vital online info with encryption so strong that it might take a hacker between decades and forever to crack. Just remember to use a strong password as the master password for the password manager.

If you are convinced, but don't know which password manager to choose, I would recommend LastPass or DashLane. (Full disclosure, I have no affiliations with either company.) These are the two that we recommend to our clients, and use in-house at Red Five. Both are easy to install and use. It just depends on your personal preference.

You don't always need to provide your SSN

It's true! SSNs were never intended to be a personal identifier, but that is exactly what they've become in the U.S. without the existence of a national identity registration system (like they use in most European countries).

There are certain times when SSNs must be used. For instance, in most financial transactions that involve the issuance of credit (e.g. applying for a loan, lease or credit card), or the opening of financial accounts (e.g. savings, checking, investing). The same is true for employment records, tax returns (both federal and state), applications for Medicare or Social Security benefits, and in certain states, applications for hunting, fishing or other recreational use licenses.

One of the most common myths is that you're required to use your SSN every time you check-in for a doctor's appointment. This is not the case. If your doctor is asking for a SSN, ask if they really need it. Chances are they don't, especially if you need a simple procedure and there's no Medicare claim. Your insurance ID number should be enough. This is true for dentists as well.

Why does this matter? Beth Givens, director of the Privacy Rights Clearinghouse, says there is "a significant amount of evidence showing ID theft cases emanate from medical offices." Research published in the JAMA Internal Medicine journal backs up this claim.

The 2018 Identity Theft Study from Javelin Strategy & Research found for the first time, thieves stole more SSNs than credit card numbers.

SSNs are taken in more than **70% of hospital data breaches** and SSNs are included in **54% of all data breaches**.

What can you do?
Next time, ask why your SSN is needed. Is there a law or requirement that says you must provide a SSN, and if so, what is it? What will happen if you don't provide it?

In some cases, your doctor may say they need your SSN because they have a field in their computerized medical records that must be filled in. The solution? Ask them to use zeros or sequential numbers 1-9.

If they tell you it's so they can track you down in case of billing or insurance problems, offer an alternative number, such as your cell phone. Giving out your cell phone number is a much more effective means for tracking you down to discuss a billing or insurance question.

The same goes for populating forms with your child's SSN. Schools, pre-schools, camps and other child-oriented businesses rarely need SSNs.

When in doubt, ask why.

KNOW THE
'SEARCHABLE' YOU

Your online reputation is often the 'first look' others get and you want it to be, at a minimum, accurate, if not totally stellar.

Potential employers and colleges often check candidate social media activity as part of the application process, and routinely consider that information in determining whether to admit a student or hire an employee. They can look for content that you've posted recently, as well as comments or photos that you may have posted years ago.

> **F**act: Over half of employers have found social media content that caused them not to hire a candidate, according to a 2018 CareerBuilder study.

What can you do?
Google yourself. See what's out there. Is it accurate? Do you make a good impression?

If you haven't already done so, enhance the privacy settings on all of your social media accounts, even ones you may not have used since high school or college. If you don't want to keep the old accounts, delete them.

If friends have posted photos of you that you don't want online (or in most cases, didn't know were online), ask them to remove them. Same goes for photos posted from schools, employers, etc. There is no guarantee that they will, but it's a good place to start.

THE TRUTH ABOUT SECURITY QUESTIONS

We all dread the inevitable automated prompt to set up those pesky security questions even though we know they are working to protect our privacy. Am I right?

But did you know you don't have to answer security questions truthfully? In fact, it's an additional safeguard to protect your digital identity.

What can you do?
Get creative. Give answers that you will remember, but are more complex for someone to hack. For instance "D0ct0r" instead of "Doctor" in response to, "What did you want to be when you were a kid?" You don't want to provide an answer that someone could easily guess or hack.

DOUBLE THE AUTHENTICATION, DOUBLE THE SECURITY

Sometimes, more is definitely more. And this holds true when it comes to two-factor authentication (2FA). Whether it's a built-in requirement or not, it's a good idea to adopt it across online services, including Twitter, Google and Facebook. Seriously, if you only do one thing, enable 2FA on all your financial and personal accounts.

Basically, 2FA is an additional security layer for you helping to address the vulnerabilities of a standard password-only approach. 2FA requires the user to have two out of three types of credentials before being able to access an account.

So how does 2FA work? With 2FA, you log into your account as you normally would. You will then receive a prompt asking you for an additional piece of information, usually a security code. If you enabled the texting feature found in most 2FA applications, you will receive that information via text within seconds of receiving the prompt. Simply enter the security code you receive via text and you are good to go. Account access granted.

The key behind 2FA is that it requires you to have access to something else in your possession that hackers won't — in this case a security code sent to your cell phone. If a hacker knows your email address and steals your common password, they still won't likely have access to your cell phone and get the security code when they try logging in.

What can you do?
Use it. Always. The extra second or two it takes to authenticate is worth it in order to protect your online accounts.

You're only as secure as your weakest link

You don't have to use the wireless router and Wi-Fi device from your internet provider. Using a third-party device may be more work to set up, but it is more secure, and provides additional features to secure a home network.

Why is this important? Cybercriminals can access your home network though your router. It happened in 2018 when cybercriminals accessed routers through the VPNFilter Malware that infected over half a million routers in more than 50 countries. The VPNFilter hack was able to install malware on to devices and systems allowing safe communication between connected devices and the internet.

Malware can make your router inoperable. It can also collect information passing through your router, block network traffic and steal your passwords.

What can you do?

It takes a little more time and effort to purchase and install a third-party internet router, but is well worth the tradeoff given the enhanced security. Buy a separate home Wi-Fi router like Google Home or Netgear Orbi and and follow their instructions for set up. Make sure you use a strong password when setting up the password.

If you don't want to purchase and install a third party internet router you can change the default login password that's used to manage your home router and Wi-Fi. Get the technician to help you change it when they are installing the router and Wi-Fi. If your router and Wi-Fi are already installed, call your internet provider to obtain the password and instructions on how to change it.

LEGAL DOCUMENTS ARE
YOUR FRIENDS

You might consider legal documents a hassle, an unnecessary expense, or even a bit too formal for establishing everyday relationships with those close to you. But what these documents aim to do is provide clarity and security in life's gray areas.

I like to think of non-disclosure agreements or confidentiality agreements like a Will. It is incumbent on you (and the responsible thing to do) to plan for life's unexpected outcomes, so your loved ones feel protected. It's the same way if your nanny is with your child 12 hours every day — you want to be confident that this employee is not jeopardizing your information, property or child's security.

When there's a tidy agreement in place, it prevents future messes and provides peace of mind.

What can you do?

Establish non-disclosure agreements and confidentiality agreements with caretakers and others that have unfettered access to your home and your children.

DON'T LET YOUR DEVICES OUTSMART YOU

Everyday devices, many of which we can't live without, comprise the "Internet of Things" (IoT) and may expose your personal data and conversations to hackers, government agencies and other third-party actors.

Most IoT devices are vulnerable to malware, as most devices have little to no built-in security. Why? Because the security features aren't often a top priority for the manufactures. Convenience tends to trump security in consumer goods. They also come with default or hardcoded passwords that can be easily obtained via a quick internet search.

A quick Google search for "Samsung Smart TV Password" produced the following in under .75 seconds:

"What is the default password for Samsung Smart TV? Enter your TV's security PIN. The default PIN is 0000; however, if you had previously changed it, enter the new PIN."

That was a piece of cake.

A hacker could easily access your home network absent a secure password on your smart TV. (And let's be honest, setting a TV password is typically not the first thing anyone does when setting up a new TV.)

What can you do?
- Set a strong password on your Wi-Fi network and use separate strong passwords on all your devices. (See Chapter 8 for more on creating passwords.)
- Create a guest network for friends and visiting family to use.
- Install software updates as they become available.

Digital assistants, such as Alexa, Google Home, Siri, etc., collect information about your habits and lifestyle. The presence of voice-enabled devices throughout your home creates a network of "hot mics" — the perfect opportunity for adversaries to surreptitiously eavesdrop on your private conversations.

"Always listening" devices could also be exploited by hackers to access your device's microphone and discretely record your conversations. The presence of the microphone in these voice-assisted devices creates the potential for hackers to turn your virtual assistant into a listening device without your knowledge.

Digital assistants are specifically designed to be a central control hub for a number of other "smart home" devices — such as lights, refrigerators and security cameras. All of these devices — many of which have weaker security protocols than virtual assistants — can be potential points of vulnerability where hackers could penetrate your network.

The bottom line is the more interconnected your listening device is to your other home systems, the more vulnerable it becomes.

What can you do?
While the most effective way to avoid compromising your personal data and conversations due to a virtual assistant is not to use one, there are methods to help limit exposure to hackers.

- Purchase a virtual assistant with a mute button and use it during sensitive discussions. Hackers could unmute the device without your knowledge, so for truly confidential discussions, unplug the device.
- Hold sensitive discussions in a designated room from which the device cannot pick up your voice. Most digital assistant devices are designed to hear a voice from a substantial distance.

- Regularly delete the logs of your requests from your digital assistant to limit the amount of personal information available for compromise.
- Regularly change the passwords on every device that you connect to your home network, so that it no longer uses the default.

EPILOGUE

Professionally, I have spent a great deal of time educating individuals and families about what is at stake and how to protect their privacy and data. I hear a lot of, "Wow, I had no idea," and, "I wish I had known about these simple security steps sooner."

Protecting your privacy is not hard. It is very doable. It takes conscious thought, a little action and a lot of discipline. Over time it becomes like any other good habit — something you do without thinking.

Personally, I have started to teach my family how to practice good cyber-hygiene, how to protect their privacy, and how to be conscientious users of technology. One of my prouder parenting moments came earlier this year when I received a call from a fellow parent. My daughter and her friend had been at a party where group pictures were taken. My daughter piped up and "informed" the parent in charge that she couldn't post any pictures of her online — and if she had to take pictures of them, take the pictures from behind and, according to my daughter, 50 feet away. (She added the last part herself.)

The reason I am sharing this story is to show that anyone can be an advocate for their privacy, and more of us should. It is your privacy, only you can protect it.

REFERENCES

1 http://www.ncsl.org/research/telecommunications-and-information-technology/security-breach-notification-laws.aspx

2 https://www.washingtonpost.com/technology/2019/04/10/tracking-your-pregnancy-an-app-may-be-more-public-than-you-think/?utm_term=.932400a831da

3 https://www.washingtonpost.com/technology/2019/04/10/tracking-your-pregnancy-an-app-may-be-more-public-than-you-think/?utm_term=.932400a831da

4 https://www.cnn.com/2019/04/22/uk/most-common-passwords-scli-gbr-intl/index.html

5 https://www.cnn.com/2019/04/22/uk/most-common-passwords-scli-gbr-intl/index.html

6 https://thycotic.force.com/support/s/article/Calculating-Password-Complexity

7 https://random-ize.com/how-long-to-hack-pass/

8 https://www.consumerreports.org/digital-security/everything-you-need-to-know-about-password-managers/

9 http://www.nbcnews.com/id/12137393/ns/business-consumer_news/t/who-can-ask-your-social-security-number/#.XbhwqS3MxZ0

CPSIA information can be obtained
at www.ICGtesting.com
Printed in the USA
LVHW080557100320
649512LV00001B/1/J